Where Do All The Lost Socks Go?

A Comedy of Missed Opportunities

Wm. Matthew Graphman

authorHOUSE®

AuthorHouse™
1663 Liberty Drive
Bloomington, IN 47403
www.authorhouse.com
Phone: 1 (800) 839-8640

Published by AuthorHouse 04/27/2016

ISBN: 978-1-5246-0557-5 (sc)
ISBN: 978-1-5246-0556-8 (e)

Print information available on the last page.

Any people depicted in stock imagery provided by Thinkstock are models, and such images are being used for illustrative purposes only. Certain stock imagery © Thinkstock.

This book is printed on acid-free paper.

Because of the dynamic nature of the Internet, any web addresses or links contained in this book may have changed since publication and may no longer be valid. The views expressed in this work are solely those of the author and do not necessarily reflect the views of the publisher, and the publisher hereby disclaims any responsibility for them.

www.matthewgraphman.com

Performance Requirements

This product is provided as a reader copy only. This product is intended to be used for personal entertainment or assessment of production viability. No portion of this product may be used in actual performance preparation without first securing a performance license from the author.

Performance License: $25.00 First Performance / $10.00 Additional Performance

To request a performance contract, please contact the author via email at: mgraphman@yahoo.com or by mail at: 1088 W. Burma Rd. Bloomington, IN 47404

Cast of Characters:

- Emma – Elderly woman, and owner of the Missing Right Sock Laundry
- Tracy – Younger woman and counter clerk at the laundry
- Charles Randolph (Chuck) – Young boy who frequents the laundry to play the aging pinball machine and occasionally help out
- Bob – Maintenance guy for the laundry – middle aged and a bit cranky
- Swifty (Robber) – A lone bank robber, on the loose trying to hide from the police
- Sandy – Police woman who uses the laundry and is a regular
- Erin – Charles mom and regular at the laundry, she is single.
- Mr. Tom Eccleston - The bank manager

Synopsis:

Ms. Emma runs a small laundry known in the community as the "Lost Sock." She has a lot of regular customers and her staff is top of the line, but some recent issues with the bank has left her and her employees with some doubts about the future of the laundry. News around town spreads of a recent robbery. And in comes a stranger who carries with him a bag full of questions. Ms. Emma in a last ditch effort to save her precious Laundromat has purchased a new super-sized machine to help the community with their large volume laundry needs.

All of this cultivates into a hilarious look at how life brings us all kinds of opportunities, some of which we take and others we miss completely.

Setting:

Inside the "Lost Sock Laundry".

Stage:

The stage is partitioned in the middle by a serving window which separates the Laundromat from the office area. SL is the main entrance. At center stage is the newly installed Wash-O-Matic, and adjacent to that is the entrance to the maintenance room behind the machines. Beside the serving window is the ancient pinball machine. Inside the office are desk and chairs, a computer and a door leading off to storage closet.

OUTLINE

Act 1

Act 2

Directors Notes:

This play is designed to work either as a stand-a-lone drama or as a larger dinner theater style production. The activities included support the dinner theater implementation and should not be considered for a dramatic performance. The alternate endings can be utilized in either type of performance. The director should consider before the start of rehearsals how to handle the various endings. If the director chooses to incorporate both endings, they should be implemented on a performance by performance basis. It is not recommended that both endings be performed on a single given performance. Using the break between Acts, the director could petition the audience to the style of ending they wish to see. This can be handled through the question: Is Swifty a robber? The answer would then drive which ending the audience should see.

Dinner Theater:

Order of Events

Times below are suggestions.

Doors Open – Seating Begins (15 – 30 minutes)

Dinner is Served (45 minutes to 60 minutes)

Act 1 Scene 1

Sock Mismatch Game (10 minutes)

Act 1 Scene 2

Dessert is Served, Ballot for Ending Choice (20 - 30 minutes)

Act 2 Scene 1

Clothes Basket-ball Game (10 minutes)

Act 2 Scene 2

If Swifty is Robber

Washingmachine Relay Game (5 minutes)

Act 2 Scene 3

ACT 1
Scene 1

It is early morning at the laundry. When the scene opens, the audience will notice that the stage is broken into two sections separated by service window and partial wall. The one side – stage left - is the customer side building. This area contains many washing machines, benches or chairs for patrons; a few tables with magazines scattered on them; a bookshelf with miscellaneous books, puzzles and games to help pass the time; an old pinball machine is positioned in the corner of the stage; in the center of the back wall is an appliance tarp covering up a newly arrived machine. The door going out to the street displays a "Help Wanted" sign. A television is offstage in the direction of the audience and several of the chairs should be set pointed in the general direction for the cast to monitor the news.

The stage right half of the set is the back office to the Laundromat. Here is a desk complete with a desktop computer some chairs and a filling cabinet. The office side of the set has one main exit –stage right – that leads off to a storage area. There is a swinging door in the wall between the customer side and the office side of the stage.

{Emma appears outside the street door of the laundry and fishes around inside a ragged old purse looking for the door keys. After fidgeting around with the lock, she lets herself into the laundry. As she crosses the customer side of the stage she is careful to straighten up the magazines as she is humming along merrily to herself. Emma crosses through the swinging door into the office area and grabs a remote control off of the corner of the desk. She leans out the service window and clicks the remote towards the audience.}

TV Voice 1: Stop by the Fuzzy Friends animal shelter and check out Snowball along with all of her furry companions and see if any of them would make a fantastic addition to your family.

TV Voice 2: Thanks for that update. Coming up next, but first this just in, an announcement was made by the estate of the late philanthropist Rex Oxnard. One of the several designees to receive a large distribution of the former millionaires' estate has been found. The individual's identity has not been disclosed, but sources indicate the recipient received a cash settlement to the tune of two hundred and fifty thousand dollars. Up next, an interview with one of Morgantown's oldest and well know entrepreneurs and some exciting news about a new service that the "Missing Sock Laundry" will be making available to the community.

Emma: Oooow, this is so exciting. {She crosses back into the customer area and walks over towards the appliance tarp} Bob.{Pause, no response} Bob, I know you're back there. How's it coming?

Bob: {From offstage behind the machines} Oh, good morning Miss Emma. I didn't hear you come in. Just a few more todos and we should be ready to go.

Emma: Well, you need to drop what you're doing and come out here. I don't want you to miss my big TV interview with the Eyeball Morning News.

Bob: {Clanking of a wrench can be heard} Oh, is that on. {A smacking sound is heard as Bob cracks a knuckle on the pipes} Ow, wow!

Emma: Bob, what did you do?

Bob: {Enters through the maintenance door to face Emma. Bob is rubbing his hand} Just a little slip of the wrench, Miss Emma. Nothing these knuckles haven't had happen to them countless times before, it's just that initial smart that catches you off guard. That thing has more hoses and connections than half the machines in this shop put together.

Emma: You love it and you know it.

{Tracy appears in the door of the laundry and enters}

Tracy: Good morning, Miss Emma. Good morning, Bob.

Emma & Bob: Good morning, Tracy.

Emma: Tracy, you're just in time for the big interview on the Eyeball morning news.

Tracy: Don't just stand there turn it up.

TV Anchor: Joining us now is Miss Emma Trowbridge of the Lost Sock Laundromat, good morning.

Tracy: Look there you are!

TV Emma: Good Morning.

Emma: {to Tracy} What do you think of my hair?

Tracy: {Looking at Emma} It looks fine, Miss Emma.

Emma: Not me now, on TV.

Tracy: Oh, it's . . . different.

Bob: Would you two be quiet**?**

Emma & Tracy: Sorry.

TV Anchor: So, what's this big announcement that you have for the community?

TV Emma: Well, pretty soon we're going to be offering a new service to the community that hopefully will be filling a gap that we've had for a long time.

TV Anchor: Tell me more. How did you identify this gap?

Tracy: {To Emma} Gap?

{Emma waves towards the TV}

TV Emma: Some extensive market research has shown that this area has a desperate need for large object facilities.

Tracy: {To Emma} Large object, what?

Emma: That's okay, he didn't get it either.

TV Anchor: I'm sorry; you'll have to be a little more basic for me. I'm just a reporter and I don't understand all of the inner workings of the laundry business.

TV Emma: First all, we don't call it the laundry business.

Emma: Listen to this. Listen.

TV Emma: It's the Universal Fabric Maintenance and Restoration Service. UFMRS pronounced oof-mars, is a highly specialized segment of the economy that supports a wide range of consumers.

Bob: Oof-mars, I like the sound of that.

TV Anchor: I see, so how does this large object facility assist the wide range of consumers in the oof-mars industry.

Tracy: Nice recovery.

TV Emma: Well put. Essentially, it means that we can now provide our patrons the ability to launder large or bulky objects such as carpets, large bed spreads, curtains and the like.

Bob: That is if I ever get that thing hooked up.

Emma: I have faith you'll get it.

TV Anchor: And your marketing research indicated that this was something that the community needed?

TV Emma: Yes, it showed there was a desperate need.

Tracy: {To Emma} Market research! What market research?

TV Anchor: Did you use a high powered marketing firm to help you gather this information that lead to your decision.

TV Emma: Oh no, we conducted all of the marketing internally.

Tracy: You did what?

Emma: We did too.

Tracy: Ms. Emma. I'm here just as much as you are any more, and I don't recall doing any market research before you up and said we needed to buy that honking behemoth of a washing machine over there.

Emma: Now Tracy, don't get your blood pressure up, but I have been asking several of our patrons for some time what they wanted that would help improve our service offerings.

Tracy: You call that market research?

Emma: I most certainly do.

Tracy: And can you name any of those {using air quotes} patrons?

{Erin and Chuck enter, chuck is carrying a large sack of laundry}

Emma: Here comes one of them right now.

Erin: Morning, Ms. Emma. Tracy, Bob. How are you doing today?

{Chuck drops the laundry sack near a washing machine}

Tracy: Oh, we're just watching Ms. Emma on the morning news give an interview.

Bob: And discussing the finer points of market research.

Erin: Oh, that's nice.

Emma: Good morning, Charles Randolph.

Chuck: Good morning, Ms. Emma. {To Mom} Can I have a quarter?

Erin: May I have a quarter.

Chuck: Yes, mom, may I have a quarter?

Emma: {Pulling a quarter out of her pocket} Here you go, Charles. First one's on me.

{Chuck reaches out and hesitates to take it, then looks at his mom who nods approvingly}

Erin: What do you say?

Chuck: Thank you, Ms. Emma. {Chuck bows like a gentlemen and then heads over to the pinball machine}

Emma: Your very welcome, sir.

Erin: So, what is this about marketing research?

Bob: We were just discussing here after watching Ms Emma on TV . . .

Erin: You are on TV?

Tracy: She most certainly is {points out to the TV}

Erin: What's wrong with it?

Emma: Oh, it does that flickering thingy when I paused it. DVRs are wonderful invention aren't they?

Bob: As I was saying, Ms. Emma got on the Eyeball Morning news and was talking a little bit about our latest addition. {He steps back and sweeps his arms towards the direction of the Wash-O-Matic 3000}

Erin: Oooh, what's that?

Bob: It's the GP Wash-O-Matic 3000, super capacity washer and dryer.

Chuck: Wow, you mean that thing washes and dries at the same time?

Bob: No, but it will do both.

Erin: It looks big.

Emma: Its one of the largest production laundry machines in the world.

Tracy: Which brings us back to the Marketing research that was done that inspired Ms. Emma to acquire such a massive machine.

Erin: I'm very interested in market research, that's part of what I do for a living.

Emma: I didn't know that.

Bob: Well, if you all are gonna start talking business, I best get back to hooking up ol' Curiosity.

Tracy: Curiosity? What's Curiosity?

Bob: {Smiling} Exactly. {Exits though maintenance door}

Tracy: Did I miss something?

Emma: Erin, what do you have to do with Marketing?

Erin: I help out with surveys that our firm puts out. I compile the data that gets collected and I try to identify core demographics that could be impacted by implementing various strategies that are targeted to those statistics.

Emma: {A bit overwhelmed by her response} Oh.

Tracy: Would you quit changing the subject, I want to know what "marketing research" you did that inspired you to purchase that machine that Bob is quickly falling in love with.

Emma: {struggling} I . . . um compiled some data from a set of demographic surveys that showed me statistics of various strategies.

{Erin begins to snicker}

Tracy: Just as I thought, you didn't do any market research. You got sold that machine by some slick young salesman.

Emma: No really, I asked questions. {pause – looking to Erin for help} To lots of people. {pause} Like Erin here.

Tracy: Really?

Erin: I don't remember you ever asking me any questions?

Emma: Oh, you remember. About 2 months ago, you came in here all upset because Charles Randolph had spilled some chocolate milk on your rug in the living room, and no matter how hard you tried you couldn't clean it with a towel. You said you hated to go and rent a steam vac for just a simple little job and you wished that I had a machine big enough to throw it in like you would your laundry.

Erin: Oh, yeah, I remember that now.

Chuck: {Calling from the pinball machine} It wasn't all my fault. The cat knocked it off the coffee table.

Tracy: But Emma, that's not market research.

Emma: It is too.

Erin: Tracy, I'm afraid Ms. Emma may be on to something. Picking up on customer needs is a form of market research.

Tracy: Oh come on, Erin.

Erin: No really, but you would need more than just my problem to justify it.

Emma: And there was.

Tracy: Like . . .

{Emma points as Sandy enters carrying a bag of laundry}

Sandy: {Reacting to stares of everyone and Emma's pointed finger in a "Don't Shoot" stance} Whatever it was, I didn't do it, Ms. Emma, honest.

Tracy: Maybe you can clear something up for us.

Erin: {Moving to a set of machines} Chuck, honey. Please come help me get this started.

Chuck: Okay. I just finished. {Crosses with Erin to beside a set of machines. They begin sorting laundry into two separate units while Tracy, Emma and Sandy discuss things}

Sandy: First things first, I'm going to need some change. {Pulls out a 20 dollar bill} Can you break this for me please?

Tracy: {Taking the bill} No problem. {Cross back into the office and begins getting change out of their cash box}

{Director's Note: Please be careful of the placement of the twenty dollar bill. This can easily be confused with the fakes that will be discovered later. It is important that audience do not confuse this bill with the fakes in order to avoid suspicion of the officer as a counterfeiter.}

Emma: Are you working today?

Sandy: Always. I'm pulling a double today. I got K9 patrol today, but I needed to drop some stuff off. You wouldn't mind running it through the cycles for me would you?

Emma: No, that's not a problem

{There's a loud crash}

Bob: {From off stage} I'm all right!

Sandy: Bob you better be careful. I don't want to have come back there and rescue your hide.

Bob: Is that Sandy?

Sandy: Who else?

Bob: Don't even think about stepping back here. You'll get yourself killed or worse. You might break something in my sophisticated network of . . .

Sandy: Oh be quiet.

Tracy: Don't mind him, he's just being a little over protective.

Sandy: What about?

Tracy: His new toy.

Bob: I heard that, it's not a toy.

Sandy: Cool it, Bob, I'm talking to the ladies.

Emma: It's our newest addition. The GP Wash-O-Matic 3000.

Chuck: It washes and dries at the same time!

Emma: Not exactly, it's a large capacity unit that washes and dries, but not at the same time.

Sandy: That's nice.

Emma: And you are partially to blame for it.

Sandy: I am, how?

Tracy: I can't wait to hear this one. I'm sure it has something to do with her {air quotes} market research.

Emma: You came in here several weeks ago, right after you got on with the K9 unit.

Sandy: Ok.

Emma: Anyway, right after you got your dog, Fluffy . . .

Sandy: Ms. Emma, his name is Stephán.

Emma: Oh, yes, Stephan. My memory is just not what it used to be. {Drifts off into forgetfulness}

Sandy: {Trying to revive the conversation} You were saying.

Emma: You came in with Fluf . . Stephán and commented about how you'd just bought him his own neat little bed.

Sandy: Yes, I remember that. But how does that qualify as market research or better yet, make me to blame for you buying a monster machine.

Emma: Sandy, you also mentioned that while you liked the soft fluffy bed – oh, now I know why I thought of Fluffy – you were wondering how you were going to keep it clean.

Tracy: Oh, I get it. You took her moment of consideration and turned that into market research.

Sandy: How thoughtful.

Emma: Thank you.

Sandy: Let me know when it's ready, cause Fluffy . . . I mean Stephán's bed is starting to smell. I give him a bath pretty regularly, but dogs are still dogs. And that bed is not the smallest thing in the world. It wouldn't fit in a normal washing machine.

Emma: Bob is working hard to get it up and running just as soon as possible.

Sandy: So in other words, don't hold my breath.

Bob: I heard that!

{Ladies all share a laugh}

Sandy: I see you put that help wanted sign up in the window.

Tracy: Yeah, that's another one of her ideas.

Emma: I'm not as much help as I used to be around here, and I'm trying to bring in a trainee so that Tracy can have someone to help carry the load out here on the floor.

Tracy: I keep telling her, I'm fine and that she does plenty. We're a good team.

Emma: That we are, Tracy, but I think you need a break once in a while, and I just can't do it on my own.

Sandy: Any qualifications in particular you're looking for?

Emma: I don't know.

Tracy: Well for one, they need to be able to handle money. We don't need someone who can't at the very least make change and work a cash register.

Erin: It might be a good idea to have someone that knows a little bit about laundering in general. You know, the basics like how to separate lights from colors. Hot from cold and what temperature the drying cycle should be set at.

Sandy: Well, make sure you have me do a security check on them for you. I don't want some hooligan taking advantage of you.

Tracy: It would also be helpful if that person knew a little about plumbing or electrical work; so that they could help Bob out on occasion.

Bob: {From in back, poking his head outside the utility door} Hey, I like that idea. And while you're at it, make sure they have a sunny disposition.

Sandy: What? Like yours?

Bob: Couldn't hurt.

Chuck: He needs to know how to work on pinball machines, too.

Tracy: Why, is something broken?

Chuck: No, not really. I just haven't been able to break one hundred thousand points yet today and win a free game.

Emma: Slow down, I can't remember all of these details. Wait just a second while I go get a piece of paper and a pen to write this all down.

Tracy: I'll help you.

{A police radio tone is heard}

Sandy: Excuse me just a second, Ms. Emma? {Stepping away, and activating the microphone on her uniform} This is Sandy? {She holds her hand up to her ear piece to listen in}

{Tracy steps out of the office area with a pen and notepad}

Emma: Thank you, dear. Now, where were we.

Sandy: {Still to the microphone} Roger that, ETA is 10 minutes.

Tracy: What's up?

Sandy: Sorry, I gotta run. A robbery just took place across town at the People's Republic Bank.

Emma: You hurry on off, I'll make sure your stuff gets taken care of. You just come back and get it after you catch that no good burglar. I'm confident you and Fluffy will track the bad guy down in no time.

Erin: I'm glad I bank at Washington Bank.

Sandy: Thank you. {As she exits}

Tracy: It's Stephán.

Emma: How do you know the burglar's name is Stephán?

Tracy: Her dog's name is Stephán.

Emma: Oh, I know that.

{End Scene 1}

Act 1
Scene 2

An hour or so has passed. Erin is seated on one of the benches knitting or sowing. Chuck is seated next to her reading a book. Tracy is seated at the desk in the office working on paperwork on the computer and Emma is standing at the customer window on the customer side leaning in going over her list of qualifications for a new employee.

Emma: I think I have it now.

Tracy: Great, we've only went over it 4 times.

Emma: Just you wait, young lady. One of these days, you'll be a silver haired goddess like me and things won't stick so quickly in the gray matter.

Tracy: Oh, I believe it. Why just the other day, I was heading out to the car to come in to work. And I sat down in the car and closed the door when I realized that I had forgotten my lunch. So I got up and went back into the house to get my lunch, and I realized that I hadn't made my lunch yet. So, I started to pull some stuff out of the refrigerator to make my lunch, when I remembered, I didn't need lunch because you were bringing in your special roast and spatzil.

Emma: Why were you telling me all this?

Tracy: Because you'd just admonished me about how getting older, you tend to forget things.

Emma: {Teasing} Oh. Is that what I was doing?

Tracy: {Playing along} Stop that.

Emma: Okay, so let's see if I have this all down . . .

Tracy: NOOOOO! Erin, help me, please!

Erin: {Setting her knitting or sowing down} Let's see what you got, Ms. Emma.

{Emma hands her list over to Erin}

Erin: Money . . . okay, laundry . . .good. Very personable – I like that.

Chuck: What about pinball repairman?

Erin: Hmm, let me see. {Scans the list} Nope, didn't make the cut.

Chuck: Aw, why not?

Emma: Couldn't afford it.

Chuck: What do you mean?

Emma: People with those skills will want way more than I'll be able to afford to pay them.

Chuck: Really?

Emma: Besides, Charles, you wouldn't want someone coming in here that knows more about that pinball machine than you. They'd liable to take over all of your high scores.

Chuck: I hadn't thought about that. Mom, if you see anything about video game mechanic or pinball expert on that paper, go ahead and cross it off for Ms. Emma. I've got that covered.

Erin: I'll just jot down here. "No pinball expertise needed or desired."

{Bob enters the room from the maintenance area}

Chuck: {See's Bob and runs over to him} Bob, we just avoided a total disaster.

Bob: Really, what happened?

Chuck: We almost had Ms. Emma hire a pinball wizard and then I would have been out of a job.

Bob: We got that stopped, didn't we? {Looks up at the ladies with fain concern}

Chuck: Yeah, mom's even put into the job description no pinball experience wanted, or something like that.

Bob: Well, I would say that we nearly avoided a total catastrophe. But . . . oh you're not concerned.

Chuck: What is it?

Bob: I was just thinking, you could be missing out on a great opportunity here.

Chuck: Really, how?

Bob: Now, I know you're hotshot on that pinball machine. But what if Ms. Emma hired someone who was even better than you are.

Chuck: That's what I'm afraid of.

Bob: Ah, you don't need to be afraid of that. As one of Ms. Emma's favorite customers, I'm sure she'd have a word with the individual – and before long he'd be showing you all of his tricks, and you'd get even better!

Chuck: I don't know, you think he'd share his secrets.

Bob: If Ms. Emma instructed him to, he'd most certainly have too. You'd be missing out on a great opportunity.

Chuck: I need to give it some thought, over a game of pinball. {Runs over to the pinball machine}

Tracy: How's it coming, Bob?

Erin: Yes the suspense is killing me.

Bob: Then you need wait no longer, the GP Wash-O-Matic 3000, is now fully operational. Curiosity is ready to roll – in a manner of speaking.

{Bob crosses over to the big machine and pulls back the covering to review a large front loading washing machine with an extra-wide door.}

Erin: Curiosity?

Tracy: That's what I said.

Emma: Oh, pay no mind to Bob. He gives all our machines names. He says it helps build a special bond between mechanic and machine. Makes it easier to fix what's wrong, I guess.

Bob: {Grinning and petting his new machine} What do you think?

Erin: Curious.

Bob: No, Curiosity?

Erin: Sorry, that's not what I meant. I was just curious – I mean wondering, how big that thing is.

Bob: The largest in the industry, ain't that right Ms. Emma?

Emma: Suppose to be.

{Erin crosses over to look over the machine}

Erin: Charles, come over here and look at the Curiosity.

Chuck: I don't think so, mom.

Erin: {stunned at the response} Why not?

Chuck: {With a big grin} Because, curiosity killed the cat!

Erin: Oh, get over here.

{Chuck hurries over next to his mother}

Chuck: Wow, that is big. Is it big enough for a person?

Bob: I suppose so, but I wouldn't want to be the one to go for a ride in there.

{Swifty approaches the door to the laundry and cautiously looks inside.}

Bob: So, now that you've seen the outside, would all of you like to see the real guts of the operation.

Tracy, Chuck & Erin: {In unison} Yeah, sure.

Bob: Excellent. Follow me, then. Watch your step. {To Chuck} And don't touch anything.

Chuck: Yes, sir! {Salutes}

{Swifty enters the laundry carrying a sack that looks not unlike a laundry bag and looks around as Bob, Tracy, Erin and Chuck go into the maintenance area of the laundry. Emma sees what she suspects is a customer.}

Emma: {To Bob} Bob, I'll be there shortly. {To Swifty} Can I help you, young man?

Swifty: Hi. I couldn't help but notice; you have a help wanted sign on your door.

Emma: Indeed, I do.

Swifty: If you're still looking for help, I'd like to apply for the job.

Emma: You would, wonderful.

Swifty: I'm only looking for something, part time, I hope that's okay.

Emma: I think that would be just fine. Have a seat. {Notices the laundry sack} One of the perks for working here is you can do your laundry for free.

Swifty: Huh?

Emma: Your laundry, I noticed you brought your laundry with you.

Swifty: {Realizes she noticed the sack} Oh, this. Yea, well . . . that's what brought me in here in the first place.

{Swifty sits down at the bench as Emma crosses to the customer window to grab a clipboard and pen}

Emma: Tracy says I need to have you fill this stuff out. I think it's just a waste of time and paper. I figure, the best way to hire someone is to talk with them a few minutes and then by that time, I know if they're gonna work out or not.

Swifty: Oh, yes, ma'am. I couldn't agree with you more.

{Emma hands him the clipboard anyway}

Emma: Just put your particulars there, if you don't mind. What's your name, young man?

Swifty: Swifty.

Emma: Nice to meet you, Swifty. Is that a nickname?

Swifty: Sort of, it's short for something, but it's been so long, you'd have to ask my mother what it's short for.

Emma: Does she live around here.

Swifty: {For a minute, Swifty shows some regret and emotion, but quickly resumes writing} No, I haven't seen her for a long time.

Emma: Oh, that's too bad. One of the most important people in the world, to a young man is his mother.

Swifty: Well, not for this boy. She left me on the street to fend for myself right after I got into high school. So, I've been going from place to place and job to job trying to find some hope.

Emma: That's quite a story, young man. There's always hope, you know. So long as you look to the one who provides hope.

Swifty: I'm not sure, I follow you. But with this job and a few other recent events, things might just be about ready to turn around for this rebel.

Emma: Oh, goodness, the job. Yes, I need to ask you some questions.

Swifty: Go ahead.

Emma: I got to find them first. {Emma looks around for her notepad.} Oh, where did I put that notepad.

Swifty: {Spots the notepad on top of a machine, walks over and picks it up and walks it to her} Is this what you're looking for?

Emma: Goodness gracious, thank you. Yes. Yes it is.

{Swifty crosses back to the bench to continue writing}

Emma: Now let's see. Can you handle money?

Swifty: Yeah, I have no problem with that.

Emma: Do you know how to operate a cash register.

Swifty: I've gotten into them a few times. They're all a little different, but I'm sure I can figure yours out quick enough.

Emma: Good, I like that positive attitude. {Pauses} How about laundry? Are you good with that?

Swifty: Oh, yeah. I can handle that.

Emma: Excellent, I'm really starting to like you. Let's see, what about fixing things?

Swifty: {Pauses, and thinks for a minute} I suppose you could say I'm pretty handy.

Emma: Oh, Bob will be so excited to hear that.

{Mr. Eccleston approaches the door to the laundry. As he does, Swifty notices the bag is sitting out in the open and gently slides the bag under his seat with his foot.}

Eccleston: Good morning, Ms. Emma.

Emma: {Concern comes over Emma's face} Good morning, Tom.

Eccleston: May I have a word with you, if you're not too busy.

Emma: Yes, yes, of course. {To Swifty} Just finish that up, and I'll be right with you.

{Emma and Eccleston cross over into the office area of the laundry. Emma and Eccleston sit down on opposite sides of the desk.}

Eccleston: Emma, I'm afraid I don't have very good news for you.

Emma: I don't want to hear it, Tom. Not right now.

Eccleston: But I have too. Emma, the loan we gave you a year ago, was to help you through the down time so you could make some changes and see if you could get things to work out for you here.

Emma: And we have been making changes, Tom. Business is getting better. It's just not as quickly coming back as we'd hoped it would.

Eccleston: I know that. I've seen some of the things you've done. But, the bank is expecting you to start making payments on that loan. And, I'm afraid they're not going to be small ones.

Emma: Tom, I have to pay my staff. Right now, I can just barely make payroll and feed myself. Don't do this to me.

Eccleston: Emma, I'm not doing this to you. You had an opportunity a few years ago to retire when your husband passed away with a nice little sum of money. Instead, you wanted to keep working and donated most of insurance to charity.

Emma: And what was wrong with that?

Eccleston: Well, if the economy would have stayed strong, probably nothing. You'd be doing okay by now. But it didn't. I know we can't predict things like that, but sometimes we have make decisions carefully.

Emma: I was careful. If I hadn't stepped up and donated that money to that mission; look at all of those children that would have either been turned out to the street or put into institutions.

Eccleston: I know what you did for Sonshine mission.

Emma: Instead, now there are 30 or 40 young people, in a good environment. They're with people that love them and teach them good things, like how God loves them and wants the best for them.

Eccletson: Emma, the bank is not totally oblivious to your generosity. However, you signed a contract and we are part of a larger organization. They're asking questions. They're asking ME questions, now, and I'm running out of answers.

Emma: What are my options, bankruptcy?

Eccleston: I don't know just yet. Hopefully, it won't come to that.

Emma: Pray for me Tom. I love what I'm doing. I love the people who come in here. I don't want to lose the Sock.

Eccleston: {Rising} I will, Emma. Bless your heart.

Emma: Just give me a few more weeks, please.

Eccleston: I'll see what I can do. I'll go back to the board and see how many favors people owe me and see what I can pull down for you.

Emma: Thank, you. Thank you very much.

Eccleston: Well, as much as I'd much rather stay and chat with you or play a round of hearts with you and Tracy, I need to head back to the office.

Emma: Why, what's wrong?

Eccleston: Oh, the bank got robbed today.

Emma: Oh, my.

Eccleston: More specifically, one of the ATM machines got broken into.

Emma: You know, I seem to remember Sandy mentioning something about a robbery, but I didn't realize it was your bank.

Eccleston: Yeah, I need to get back. The officers were on break, and I thought I would go for a walk to try and cheer up. Funny how I ended up here. I'm just sorry, I couldn't have brought some cheer with me.

{Emman and Eccleston head out of the office into the customer side of the laundry. Bob, Tracy, Erin and Chuck are coming back from the maintenance area}

Emma: Tom, you're always welcome here, you know that. God will figure this mess out. He doesn't make mistakes.

Eccleston: I know your right. I'm just not sure how this is all going to work out.

Emma: For our good, Tom. For our good.

{Eccleston nearly bumps into Swifty who is hunched over his paper work, trying to avoid being seen}

Eccleston: Excuse me, young man. {Waves to everyone else} Have a nice day, everyone. {Notices bank sake next to Swifty as he exits}

Tracy, Erin, Bob & Chuck: {In Unison} Bye!

Tracy: Who was that?

Chuck: He looked like a doctor?

Erin: {Lost in chit-chat with Bob} Who?

Chuck: {Pointing to Tom as he leaves the building} That man.

Emma: No, that was just a friend. He's with the bank.

Bob: Which bank?

Emma: People's Republic.

Tracy: No wonder he was in such a hurry to leave. I bet things are crazy over there today, what with the robbery.

Erin: Oh, yeah. I'd forgotten about that. {To Chuck} Okay, Charles. We need to get the laundry out of the dryer and head home. We're going to come back later this evening to try out the new machine on that rug.

Chuck: But, I wanted to play one more game of pinball.

Erin: Maybe when we come back.

{The two cross over to a machine and start pulling close out and putting them away in a bag.}

Swifty: {Stands up with paper in hand and crosses over to Emma} Here you go.

Emma: Oh, why thank you. {Begins to scan the information on the sheet}

Tracy: {To Swifty} Hi, I'm Tracy, and you are?

Swifty: Oh, Hi. The name's Swifty. Nice to meet you Tracy {reaches out to accept an offered hand shake}

Tracy: So are you here about the job?

Swifty: Yeah. I just finished up the application.

Tracy: Good. {Pause as Emma continues to read oblivious to the discussion} I don't suppose, Ms. Emma has asked you any questions.

Swifty: Oh, she asked me lots of questions. She asked me about if I've handled money, if I can make change, if I know about laundering stuff, and if I was handy.

Chuck: {Interjecting} Did she ask you if you're any good at pinball?

{Swifty looks to Bob & Tracy for clarification}

Bob: {Hand on Chuck's shoulder} This is our resident pinball wizard. Not many people like to play pinball these days and he was just curious if there was another aficionado, such as himself, applying for the job.

Chuck: African avocado?

Erin: Aficionado, someone who really knows their stuff about a particular subject.

Chuck: Oh, like I do about pinball.

Bob: Precisely.

Swifty: Well, it just so happens that I won a pinball tournament once when I was in high school. So you could say that I like to play.

Chuck: Awesome!

Tracy: Well, I guess that covers all of the bases. {Looking over at Emma who is still studying the application} Ms. Emma. You've had enough time to read the entire Old Testament.

Emma: Sorry, Tracy. I was just admiring the young man's handwriting. You don't see many individuals with this level of detail anymore. Handwriting is a dying art, you know.

Tracy: Really, let me see. {Takes the app from Emma} Wow, you're not kidding. Where did you learn to write like that?

Swifty: Growing up, I spent a lot of time going place to place. One of the folks that I stayed with was a professional lettering artist. They designed fonts and signs and things. I guess I kind of picked up a lot of their style while I was there.

Tracy: That's truly amazing. Maybe we can get you to redo our signage on the window up front, that is if Ms. Emma chooses to hire you.

Emma: Already decided. Swifty, welcome to the Lost Sock Laundry.

Everyone: Yeah. Congratulations.

{Everyone cheers, Swifty is a bit surprised and overwhelmed at first at the sign of approval}

Swifty: Thanks.

Erin: Let's go, Charles. See you later everyone. Nice to meet you, Swifty.

Chuck: Bye. {Using his best Arnold Schwarzenegger voice} I'll be back.

Bob: Come on, Emma. Let me show you our masterpiece.

Emma: Oh, yes, of course.

Bob: Swifty, let me show the boss around first and then we'll go through and do a deep dive into all of the stuff that's back there.

Swifty: Sure.

{Emma and Bob exit back into the maintenance room. Swifty and Tracy come around and sit down on the bench.}

Swifty: Wow, this neat.

Tracy: How so?

Swifty: It's the first time I've actually felt like somebody was happy to have me around.

Tracy: Trust me, working for Ms. Emma can be a blast. Don't, get me wrong, sometimes the work is hard and tedious, but she always makes you feel good about what you do, and overall the people that come in here are the best.

Swifty: That's going to be different. It was never like that in the other places I've worked.

Tracy: Emma believes that the atmosphere of a place – whether it be at home or work – gets set from the top – down. She's always positive.

Swifty: That's rare. Where does it come from?

Tracy: It's her faith. She relies on God for just about everything, and He always seems to honor her for that.

Swifty: {Feeling uncomfortable} Oh, well, I'm not a big God person.

Tracy: That's okay. Ms. Emma won't beat you up for it. But I guarantee, that if you watch her long enough, you'll be interested in figuring out how to get a little of what she has.

Swifty: You mean, money.

Tracy: No. Not money. Ms. Emma doesn't keep much money. She gives most of it away, what she doesn't need for the shop, that is. Speaking of money, I wonder what that banker was doing here.

Swifty: Oh, that. I kind of overheard something about a loan coming due.

Tracy: What? Was there more?

Swifty: Well, I feel bad, I wasn't trying to listen in or anything, but it's not like they weren't just in the other room there. But, it seems that the banker has been holding on a loan for some time, and Ms. Emma hasn't been making any payments on it. I could be wrong, but it sounds to me like she might be in trouble.

Tracy: {Trying to brush it aside} I'm sure it was nothing. If there was a problem, I'm sure she'd have already told me about it.

{Entering from the back, Bob & Emma come in}

Bob: So there you go.

Emma: Bob, you've done a great job as usual. That system looks as fine as any you've put together.

Bob: Thank you. Now, my young apprentice. Shall we dive into the depths of the beast and learn what there is to be learned?

Emma: Not so fast, Bob. Just because we hired him, doesn't mean he's started. He may have other things he needs to get done today.

Swifty: Oh, no. I'm good to start right now.

Emma: Okay then. {To Bob} Have at it, I believe is how they would say it today.

{Swifty gets up and grabs his bag from under the chair. Emblazoned on the side are the words Peoples Republic Bank}

Emma: {To Swifty} Nice bag. I didn't know the bank was giving away laundry sacks.

Swifty: Yeah, just picked it up today.

Emma: Hmm. I'll have to talk to Tom about where he gets them from.

{Swifty and Bob exit. Tracy and Emma head to office}

Tracy: Ms. Emma, what was that banker doing here?

Emma: Tracy, we need to have a talk.

{Blackout}

{End Act 1 Scene 2}

ACT 2
Scene 1

{It's early in the afternoon. Ms. Emma has stepped out to fetch some lunch for everyone. Tracy is setting at the desk somewhat in a daze, still stunned by the news that Emma and the shop are in financial trouble. Bob is coming out of the maintenance room as the scene opens.}

Bob: {Calling back to Swifty} Good work, my boy. Good work. If you want to work on cleaning out those traps for a few minutes and bag up those lost socks; then Ms. Emma should be back with lunch.

Swifty: {From the back} Sure thing, Bob.

Bob: {Crosses over to window and leans in to chat with Tracy} You know, I think that kid's going to work out pretty well.

Tracy: {Only half listening} Really?

Bob: Yeah, we were going back through some of the older connections on the dry cleaning machines that we use in the back, and he spotted a loose connection. I know we don't use those machines very much anymore, but the next time we did, we would have had chemicals all over the place, if he hadn't spotted that.

Tracy: That's great, Bob. Do you know if Sandy's laundry is finished?

Bob: Yes, ma'am. We finished it up and folded and sacked it. It's right out here next to Batman.

Tracy: We? We who? You actually helped with laundry?

Bob: Well, okay, Swifty came out and folded it after I pulled it out of the dryer.

Tracy: I was beginning to think that the world had cracked up.

Bob: {Ignoring her comment} Is Ms. Emma on her way back?

Tracy: Yes, she phoned just a moment ago. She's picked up the sandwiches and should be here in just a minute or two. She said she had a surprise for us: something to help us celebrate our new team member.

Bob: Wonderful, I wonder what it is.

Tracy: I don't know. Don't really care.

Bob: Batten down the hatches; we've got some stormy seas ahead. I know that look, Tracy. Something is going on and it's not good.

Tracy: {Pretending to be busy} I don't have time to talk about it right now, Bob.

Bob: {Leaves the window and crosses into the office. He pulls up a chair and plops down} Okay. Don't mind if I sit here until either you're caught up or lunch shows, do you?

Tracy: You can be so persistent sometimes.

Bob: Just consider it a trait of an old sailor.

Tracy: I just found out that Ms. Emma's in a bit of trouble.

Bob: Trouble? Ms. Emma? What kind of trouble could she be in?

Tracy: Financial.

Bob: Oh. How bad?

Tracy: Pretty bad. Remember that banker that was here earlier?

Bob: Yeah.

Tracy: Apparently, Ms. Emma has a pretty sizeable loan that she had to take out when the economy went bad a year or so ago. She was hoping that she'd be able to ride it out, but as you know things just haven't picked up like – well, like we all hoped they would.

Bob: Things are getting better, Tracy. What with ol' Curiosity, we should have all kinds of new business. Large capacity jobs are hard to process in these parts. Emma should have a corner on the market.

Tracy: It may be too little, too late. Tom has been holding back the bank so Emma could meet payroll, but the bulk of the loan is due and he's run out of excuses.

Bob: Got any ideas.

Tracy: No. I wish I could help, but, things are so tight right now, I've been looking at getting a second job just to make ends meet.

Bob: Not good Tracy, not good.

{Swifty enters from the maintenance area carrying two sacks.}

Swifty: Hey, Bob, I got those traps cleaned out. What should I do with these smelly socks?

Bob: {Standing and crossing over to the window} Just set them beside an open machine. We'll want to run them through. Ms. Emma likes to pair up like matches as much as she can and then give them to the mission.

Swifty: Gotcha. {Swifty is careful to set the sack of socks down beside an open machine, and then carefully places his sack at the end of the bench}

{Emma enters from the outside with a sack of sandwiches and what looks to be like a pie container}

Emma: Is anybody hungry?

Bob: You bet. {Crosses to help Emma} Let me help you with that.

Emma: Thank you, Bob.

Swifty: What's that you got there?

Emma: Something very special. Since you've joined us today, I decided to splurge a little and picked up an apple pie from the bakery. Now mind you, this is no ordinary store-bought pie. This bakery is known for miles and miles for their homemade pies. Isn't that right, Bob.

Bob: Kid, you must really, rate, because, these pies are amazing.

Emma: Tracy, can you help me get things setup back in the back.

Tracy: {Heads to the back room} Sure.

{Emma and Bob exit off to the left of the stage to go setup lunch. Swifty walks over to look over the pinball machine. Erin approaches the laundry carrying a sizeable garbage bag of laundry. She is struggling to enter the laundry. Swifty rushes over to assist.}

Swifty: Here, let me help you with that.

Erin: Oh, thank you. That's not only big, but also heavy. {Trying to remember his name} Swifty, right?

Swifty: Yeah. What have you got in there?

Erin: Well, I believe it's a candidate for the magical new monster machine over there. It's the rug from my living room that I haven't been able to clean thoroughly, and I'm hoping that Ms. Emma's machine can work a miracle. Hey, "Emma's monstrous magical miracle machine". That has the ring of an advertising tag line if ever I heard one.

Swifty: Ms. Emma's stepped into the back for some lunch, would you like me to get her so you can start on this?

Erin: Oh, no, don't bother her. I'll just leave it for now. You all can start it when you're ready to christen the machine.

Swifty: Where's your son?

Erin: Chuck's at a friend's house for a little bit. I'm running a few errands and wanted to drop this off, since I don't know how long it's going to take, I figured the sooner I got it here the better.

Swifty: I'll let them know, I'm sure we'll get it started right after lunch.

Erin: Thanks. So, how's your first day on the job?

Swifty: Oh, I'm learning a lot. Still trying to figure out everything, but I think it's gonna work out.

Erin: The gang here are real nice. They're always very helpful. You seem to fit right in.

Swifty: Thanks.

{Bob sticks his head into the office and calls out across the office}

Bob: Hey, Swifty. Can you throw those socks into Droid? Emma wants to try to pair them up later today and take them down to the mission.

Swifty: Sure thing, Bob. I'll get right on it.

Bob: Okay. {Starts to leave} Oh, as soon as you get it started, we've got a sandwich in here for you, and then "The Pie!"

{Erin, crosses over to Swifty's sack, confusing it for Bob's sack and picks it up. She carries it around and opens the machine to get it ready to pour it into a machine}

Swifty: {Still looking toward the office} So, which one of these machines is Droid? {He turns to spot Erin with his sack and rushes over and pulls it out of her hands} Hey, you don't need to do that?

Erin: {Stunned that Swifty pulled the sack out} I was just trying to help.

Swifty: That's awful nice of you, but Bob is expecting me to get this started.

Erin: {Scornfully} But you don't even know which machine is Droid.

Swifty: Sure I do, it's this one. {Points to the machine that she's standing in front of}

Erin: Wrong. This is Batman, that one is Droid. I was only going to set your bag up here so I could sort the white socks from the colored ones.

Swifty: Oh. Well, I don't want you to have to take up your time with this. I'm sure you need to get to work or back home to your family, or something.

Erin: I don't have to work until this evening, and as for my family. Well, Charles is all I have.

Swifty: I'm sorry, I just assumed you were married and . . .

{Swifty sets his sack down next to Sandy's sack and picks up the other sack of socks and starts to loading Batman}

Erin: No. Charles father and I, well, let's just say I had an opportunity to do the right thing, but I didn't. And he left me as soon as he found out Charles was on the way. I've been alone ever since.

Swifty: I know that feeling. I mean, I know what it's like to be alone.

Erin: I'm sorry, I better go. {Starts to exit}

Swifty: Look, I'm real sorry, I didn't mean to upset you.

Erin: You didn't. Honest. I just had a funny feeling and it scares me. {Exits}

Swifty: I better do something with this. {He takes his Sandy's sack and stuffs the whole thing into Droid}

{Bob enters and crosses into the customer area with a sandwich}

Bob: How's it coming?

Swifty: Okay, just finished loading the washer. Do you have any change?

Bob: No, go in there and grab some out of the cash box.

Swifty: Sure. {Bob, crosses to Droid and sets the sandwich down and starts to peek in} Its not in there, I had to use Batman.

Bob: {Closing the partially opened lid} Huh? Why Batman?

Swifty: Well, I had already loaded my stuff into droid.

Bob: Oh. That's right, I forgot that's what brought you in here in the first place. You haven't started it yet, though.

Swifty: No, I was going to ask you for some change after lunch, but we hadn't got there yet.

Bob: Sure. {Moves over to Batman and opens and inspects the contents} Looks good. Did you find the detergent?

Swifty: No.

Bob: We keep a stash in the middle draw of the filling cabinet.

Swifty: {Tries to open the drawer} It's locked.

Bob: Oh, yeah. Key's in the top desk drawer.

{Swifty fetches the key and operates the filing cabinet pulling the bottle of detergent out. He closes the cabinet and starts back into the customer area}

Swifty: Oh, almost forgot the change.

{He sets the bottle down and pulls open the cash box}

Swifty: There are no quarters.

Bob: Look under the twenties.

Swifty: {Picks up a stack of bills and instead of getting out a roll of quarters examines the top twenty} Hey, Bob.

Bob: What can't you find them? {Crosses to the window}

Swifty: No, but you may have a problem.

Bob: Why's that?

Swifty: This twenty is a fake.

Bob: You sure? How can you tell?

Swifty: Well, I've handled money before, and I know a fake when I feel one.

{Mr. Eccleston approaches the laundry from the outside. Swifty sees the banker and reacts}

Swifty: I'm just gonna run in the back and grab some mayonnaise. {Swifty exits into the back room}

Eccleston: {Entering} Excuse me, Bob, is it?

Bob: {Turning, still eyeing the twenty} Yes? Oh hi.

Eccleston: Hi, is Ms. Emma available?

Bob: Well, she's currently working on lunch right now. Oh hey, maybe you can settle an argument.

Eccleston: I doubt that.

Bob: Swifty says this twenty dollar bill is a fake. I don't believe that he can tell. What do you think?

Eccleston: {Hardly interested takes the bill out of the Bobs hand without looking at it and his expression changes} Hey, you may be right. It certainly doesn't feel right. {Studies the bill a little bit closer} I can't be one hundred percent sure, but, I would strongly agree with Swifty. Is that the new kid you hired earlier today?

Bob: Yes, it is.

Eccleston: Well, I would suggest you bring these down to the bank. We can certainly run a check against the serial numbers and verify it, but, I'd say you've got some bad bills. Any idea where you got them?

Bob: No. I don't go near the money. Too much trouble. I stick with the machines. They're at least predictable. Take Juliet over here for example.

Eccleston: I'm sorry, I don't have time to stick around and chit-chat. Please give this to Ms. Emma. It's a composite sketch that the police did of the robber. Afraid it's not very detailed, the glass on the ATM was really dirty and so the image was terrible.

Bob: Who'd have thought you'd need to hire a window man for an ATM.

Eccleston: Yeah. We're looking for a young man, early twenties, around 6 foot. That's about as best we can do at this point. {Starts to exit}

Bob: Sure thing.

{Bob crosses over to the window and sets the composite sketch on the ledge along with the twenty dollar bill. Tracy enters with a plate of pie}

Tracy: Did I hear a customer out here?

Bob: No, it was just that banker stopping by.

Tracy: What did he want?

Bob: He wanted to see Ms. Emma. They got a little information on the robber including a composite sketch.

Tracy: Really, what do they know?

Bob: Well, it's a young man, early twenties is what he said. Around six feet tall.

Tracy: Well, that's real helpful. That like narrows it down to about 30 percent of the population of this area.

Bob: Don't forget the sketch.

Tracy: {Sets her pie down on the counter and picks up the sketch. Bob immediately picks up the pie and begins eating it.} Interesting. This sort of looks familiar. {Notices Bob is eating her pie} What on earth are you doing?

Bob: Oh, sorry, was this yours.

Tracy: Yes it was, it's yours now.

Bob: I'm not very good with faces. Does it ring any bells with you?

Tracy: Maybe, but I'm not sure.

{Swifty and Emma enter both carrying pie.}

Swifty: This is excellent pie, Ms. Emma.

Emma: That bakery makes some of the best. I can't seem to duplicate it, and I've even asked them for the recipe.

Swifty: Well, thank you for getting it for us.

Emma: No problem, I'm just glad to have a nice young man like you on our team.

Bob: Ms. Emma, that banker stopped by while you were lunching.

Emma: Oh, what did he want?

Tracy: Sounds like they've got a lead on the robber at the bank.

Emma: Really?

Swifty: Really?

Bob: Yes, it's a young man in his early twenties and about 6 feet tall or so.

Tracy: They also have a composite sketch. {Starts to hand it to Emma}

Emma: A sketch, let me see. {Swifty takes it from Tracy's hands}

Swifty: May I? I know a lot of twenty something six foot tall young men in this town.

Emma: I bet you do.

Tracy: The face looks familiar, but I can't put my finger on it.

Emma: Anything else happen over lunch.

Swifty: {Glad for the diversion} Oh, yes, Erin came back in. She dropped off that large sack over there. She said we could use that as our first trial run for Curiosity.

Bob: Hot diggidy Dog. I can't wait to see what she'll do.

Emma: Are we ready to roll, with it then?

Bob: Just gotta turn on the breaker in the back and open the water valves and she'll be ready to tumble.

Tracy: Well, "water" we waiting for?

Swifty: I'll load up the machine.

Bob: I'll give you the signal when she's ready to go. {Hustles off to the maintenance room}

{Swifty crosses over to the bag and picks it up and starts works his way over to the large machine. Tracy spots the twenty on the counter}

Tracy: What's this twenty doing out?

Swifty: Oh, I almost forgot. I think that's a fake.

Tracy: A Fake!

Swifty: Yeah, it feels different than normal twenties.

Bob: {Calling from the back} Oh, by the way, that banker said we should have those twenties checked. He thinks they're fakes.

Tracy: Oh, good grief.

Swifty: Any idea where we got those?

Tracy: No, money comes in here all the time. Speaking of which, I have a whole stack back in the safe.

Emma: Oh, dear, you better go get them and I'll take them all down and have them checked out.

{Tracy exits into the storage area.}

{Emma crosses over to the window counter as Swifty loads the rug into the washing machine. Emma is finishing her pie as Sandy approaches the outside of the laundry. Swifty, spotting the police woman through the window jumps into the large washing machine and throws the rug over the top of himself.}

Sandy: Good afternoon, Ms. Emma.

Emma: Why hello, Sandy. How is your afternoon going?

Sandy: I've had worse. Has Mr. Eccleston been by?

Emma: Yes, he dropped off a sketch and details of the robber.

Sandy: Excellent. Highly unlikely that he'd come by here, but just in case, I want you to be aware of what he looks like.

Emma: I do appreciate that.

Sandy: And whatever you do, don't provoke him. We're not sure that he's dangerous, but you never can tell. This is currently just a robbery. I'd rather not make it a homicide.

Emma: You mean I can't do my jujitsu on him if he shows up? {Makes a move}

Sandy: Only if you promise not to kill him.

Emma: {Smiling} Oh, with this old body, I don't think you'd have to worry about that. To be truthful, I don't think I would be lethal to a fly.

Sandy: You'd be surprised what a move like that could do to a person. {Starts to exit} Oh, did you get a chance to run that laundry through.

Emma: Sure did. {Walks over to the machines and pick's up Swifty's sack. Swifty is watching out through the window in the washing machine with big eyes} I believe this is it.

{Bob enters}

Bob: Alright Swifty you can start it now . .{Startled to see Sandy} Oh, hello again. Anybody seen Swifty?

Emma: No he was loading up the Curiosity just a few minutes ago. {Swifty ducks back under the rug as Bob crosses over}

Bob: Hmmm. Rug appears to be in there. Door didn't close all the way. Must be a little stiff. New machines need broken in too you know. {Bob pushes on the door and it snaps shut} Well, she's ready to go. Anybody got a couple of dollars.

Sandy: {Digging in her pocket} Here, I've got a couple of ones. It will help cover the cost for doing my laundry. {Swifty stares back out and realizes what's about to happen. He sees that the door is latched.} Let me know if you see anything. I'll be back after my shift with the dog's bed. I can't wait to see what this thing can do. It smells so bad.

Bob: Bring it right in and will give it a good once over. {Bob inserts the bills into the slot and water starts jetting into the machine}

{Sandy exits, as she does, Swifty sees her leave the building and starts pounding on the door}

Emma: Do you hear something?

Bob: Oh, it's probably air in the lines. Those hi pressure jets in this thing will surly make some noise at first.

Emma: It's quite the noise.

Tracy: {Entering from the back.} Has anyone seen Swifty?

Emma: No, I thought he might be with you having some more pie.

Tracy: What's that noise? It sounds like a scream.

Bob: I was just telling Ms. Emma that this machine has some pretty high pressure jets. It's possible that there's some air in the line, being its first go round.

Tracy: Or, it's just possible that you closed Swifty in the machine. Look!

{Emma and Bob turn to look through the window to see Swifty bouncing around inside the massive machine}

Emma: Quick, Bob stop the machine.

Bob: Right on it. {Bob smashes the emergency stop button}

{The three huddle around the door as they get it open and help a now wet swifty out of the machine}

Emma: My dear boy, are you okay?

Tracy: What on earth were you doing in there?

Bob: I guess you could hide a body in there.

Swifty: {Staggering around} I think I hit my head.

Emma: At least once from the way you were thrashing around in there.

Swifty: I really need to sit down, and then we need to talk.

{Lights out, Act 2, Scene 1 Ends}

{At this point in time, it is up to the director to determine how the play is going to end. You could make it an optional ending by passing out a vote card to the audience in between Acts 1 & 2 and then tallying up the votes before the start of the second Act. It will be important to know what ending to use so that Swifty has appropriate motivation for the different conflicts in Scene 1.}

Act 2
Scene 2: Original Ending

{An hour has passed and Swifty and Emma enter from the storage room}

Emma: You're not going to hurt them, are you?

Swifty: I don't want too. But, until you get my sack back from that cop, I'm not making any promises.

Emma: I don't understand why you're doing this.

Swifty: I guess I got tired of being alone all the time and not belonging. I figured if I had some money, that some opportunities would present themselves that could change that.

Emma: Oh, if only you would let me have the opportunity to introduce you to the one who can change all of that.

Swifty: I know you mean well, but right now, I think it's probably too late for that.

Emma: It's never too late to begin a relationship with Jesus.

Swifty: I only wish I would have met you one day earlier. Things could have been different. You have all been so nice and accepting to me, I just wish there was a way to change the way things are, but there isn't.

Emma: {With hope} Oh, I'm sure we can work something out. Let me talk to the police.

Swifty: No! The only talking that's going to happen is you stalling everyone until that police woman comes back with her dog bed and my sack of money. {Erin and Chuck approach the laundry} Any word from you that sounds like you're tipping people off and I will have to hurt Tracy and Bob. I'll be listening in the back. {Exits}

Chuck: Mom, may I have a quarter?

Erin: We're only going to be a few minutes.

Chuck: That's okay, I won't use my free games that I earn. I can give those to Swifty.

Emma: Good afternoon, Erin, Charles.

Chuck: Sorry Ms. Emma, don't have time to talk, I gotta get one more game in before we go.

Emma: But you just got here.

Erin: Don't mind him. We just thought we'd swing by and see how our candidate made out in the washing machine.

Emma: Oh, I apologize, but we'd started it some time ago, but something went wrong with the machine.

Erin: Oh, no. What happened?

Emma: {Thinking to herself} Not sure exactly, but whatever happened really {pointing toward the back room} burglared it up.

Erin: That's too bad. I'm sure whatever it was, Bob will be able to get it straightened out.

Emma: Oh, I wish he could, but I'm afraid he can't right now.

Erin: Why? Where is he?

Emma: Oh, he's held up in the back.

Erin: Tracy got him busy on some new project?

Emma: {Pointing to the back} No, just held up?

Chuck: {Smacks the side of the machine} Stupid machine.

Erin: Charles, that's not how we treat others property.

Chuck: Oh, I'm sorry. It's just this thing cheated me on the last ball.

Emma: You know, Charles, I've been thinking about replacing that machine with a newer one, guess what it's called?

Chuck: Phantom of the Opera?

Emma: No, the Great Bank Robbery.

Chuck: Never heard of it.

Erin: Come on, Charles. We need to get home. Tell everyone we said 'hi'.

Emma: But your rug.

Erin: Don't worry about it. We'll pick it up tomorrow.

Chuck: Bye.

{Erin and Chuck exit, and Swifty enters from the back}

Swifty: That was a close one. You need to watch yourself, Ms. Emma.

Emma: Swifty, I really want to help you.

Swifty: You can't help me. Besides, why would you want to help me?

Emma: God commands me to love you.

Swifty: That' can't be possible.

Emma: In my own power, you're right, but with God, I can.

Swifty: I'm afraid it won't do any good. {Eccleston approaches the laundry} I'm going to stay here where I can keep a closer eye on you. No funny stuff, or there will be trouble.

Eccleston: {Eccleston enters and crosses over to Emma} Good afternoon, Ms. Emma.

Emma: {Looking more downcast} Hi, Tom. I don't suppose you have any good news for me.

Eccleston: No, I'm afraid I don't. I've exhausted all of my approaches with the board. If I don't get a commitment from you to pay at least five thousand dollars by the end of next week, they're going to start legal proceedings.

Emma: Oh, Tom. I don't know where I'll be able to come up with that kind of money in two weeks. At most I'd be able to come up with half of that.

Eccleston: I know and I'm sorry. I've done all I can. Now if you'll excuse me.

Emma: What's the rush?

Eccleston: Oh, it's this whole robbery thing.

Emma: No luck, huh?

Eccleston: We'll you saw the details we got of the camera. The police don't have anything at this point. As it is, the robber is probably 2 or 3 states away.

Emma: Oh, he could be closer than you think.

Eccleston: I wish I had your optimism. Anyway, the board has just issued a reward for leads leading to the capture of the crook. It's pretty sizeable.

Emma: Is that really necessary?

Eccleston: They seem to think so. Look, Emma. I just want to remind you that when the inevitable happens, that you know I did all I could. You're one of the nicest, Godliest people I know. I just wish the economy would have worked more in your favor than it did.

Emma: {Smiling} Oh, don't you worry about it. I'm not concerned about me, I'm just worried about Tracy and Bob. I don't know how to help them when the laundry closes down.

Eccleston: Emma, if it's any conciliation, I will do everything I can to help them find a job.

Emma: Really, that would be just darling of you.

Eccleston: Oh, and don't forget to bring those bills down so we can check those out for you.

Emma: It will have to be later, I'm being held hostage at the moment {Swifty noisily clears his throat} by this place {Emma adds}.

Eccleston: I understand.

{Eccleston exits}

Swifty: So, you're going to lose this place?

Emma: Yes, I'm afraid it's probably going to come to that, unless God intervenes with a large sum of cash.

Swifty: I don't know if God can help you, but I might be willing too.

Emma: Swifty, I can't take that money, it's not yours to give in the first place.

Swifty: How are you going to help your friends if you can't take care of yourself?

Emma: God will work it all out.

Swifty: Why do you have such a positive outlook? Everything you have will be gone in just a few days. Your business, your income, your life as you've known it will be over.

Emma: We all have our opportunities given by God to do the right thing – His way – or the wrong thing – our way. I have done, what I've done to please God. If it's time for me to give up the Sock, then I'll just have to find out what's next on God's plan for me. We all have a choice. You have a choice, and it starts with accepting who God is, and what He can do for you.

Swifty: Even a messed up kid, like me?

Emma: Swifty, God specializes in taking things that are broken, and making them better than new. That's what he does. {Sandy approaches the laundry} You better scoot. I'll do my best to get your bag back for you.

{Swifty hurries back to the office area as Sandy enters the Laundry}

Sandy: Ms. Emma, what a day, what a day.

Emma: I'm so glad you stopped by.

Sandy: You are, what for?

Emma: Well, it's very embarrassing, actually. Did you take that laundry home yet that you picked up here earlier?

Sandy: No, I haven't had time. I just threw the sack in the trunk.

Emma: I'm afraid we gave you the wrong sack. That belongs to a different customer.

Sandy: Oh, wow. Okay. Guess it's a good thing I didn't go home right away. I'd hate to be the one rummaging through some stranger's undies. {Chuckles at the remark}

Emma: {Grabbing Sandy's laundry and hands it too her} Here's your laundry.

Sandy: Thank you, again. I'll run out a grab the other one. {Takes the sack and quickly exits}

{Swifty is struggling with what to do}

Emma: {As Sandy returns} So, what brings you back in such a down mood. We were expecting you later, but with a doggy bed.

Sandy: As I said, I haven't gone home yet, because of this crazy robbery deal. Things are still a mess, and with the bank announcing a reward, everybody and their brother has been contacting the department with all kinds of useless information. I wish I had time to tell you about some of the whack jobs we have here in town looking at any opportunity to score a big reward.

Emma: I wish I could help you, but I'm afraid I . . . {Swifty enters the customer side}

Swifty: I can't let you do this.

Sandy: Oh, hi, Swifty.

Emma: What do you mean dear?

Swifty: You say, there's a reward out for information that leads to the capture of the robber.

Sandy: Sure is, a pretty nice one too.

Swifty: Ms. Emma, open that bag.

Emma: What?

Swifty: Ms. Emma, I've been given an opportunity to do something right for a change, and I'm going to take it.

Emma: {Opening the bag and looking inside} Oh, my!

Sandy: {Leans over and looks inside} Is that his?

{Emma nods in sadness}

Sandy: {With Authority} I'm afraid I need to ask you to turn around and put your hands behind your back. {Swifty obeys} You are under arrest for the robbery of the People's Republic Bank. Anything you say or do can be used against you.

{Sandy & Swifty exit the laundry. Emma is silent for just a moment}

Bob: {From the back} Uh, is there anybody out there?

{Emma jumps up and runs off stage to help them}

{Act 2: Scene 2 Ends}

Act 2
Scene 3

{A couple weeks have past. Tracy is in the office.}

Eccleston: {Enters} Good afternoon, crew of the "Lost Sock".

Tracy: Is that you Tom?

Eccleston: Well, since when have we been on a first name basis?

Tracy: Ever since your bank decided that it wasn't going to close us down?

Eccleston: Ouch, that hurt. Just to be fare, it wasn't me that was going to shut you down, it was the board. And as far as deciding to not shut you down, there was no longer a reason to shut you down.

Tracy: Likely story.

Eccleston: Honestly. I have here in my formally distraught fingers a piece of paper that I need signed by the illustrious proprietor to conclude the transaction.

Tracy: Oh, well, you may have to wait a while. She's at the hearing and who knows how long it will be before she's back.

Eccleston: Really? Why on earth did she go to that?

Tracy: Well, she felt like she needed to be there for Swifty. She feels like he's changed, and wants to try and get the court to go easy on him.

Eccleston: That woman never ceases to amaze me.

Tracy: I've been around here for quite a while, and I don't know if I've ever met anybody with as much faith as she has.

{Erin and Chuck Enter}

Erin: Hi everybody.

Tracy: Oh, hi.

Chuck: We stopped by to encourage Ms. Emma.

Tracy: I'm sure she'll appreciate that.

Erin: It's really disappointing that you meet a seemingly nice person and realize that they've committed such a terrible crime.

{Emma enters}

Emma: What's this I hear about terrible crime.

Erin: Hi, Ms. Emma. I was just saying how surprised I was to see such a nice guy turn out to be a criminal.

Emma: I know it seems like what he did was bad. In man's economy it is, but in God's economy it's no different than any other sin. God is gracious to give us all opportunities to repent. I think Swifty deserved the same kind of opportunity.

Erin: I guess I never looked at it that way.

Tracy: So, how did the hearing go?

Emma: Well, there's good news and bad news.

Chuck: Let's hear the bad news first.

Emma: Well, the judge sentenced him to five years. The good news is he suspended all but 1 year of it. He'll have to spend 6 months in jail, and then he'll spend the next 6 months on work release,.

Tracy: Huh, I wonder where they're planning on placing him on work release.

Emma: Well, you could say I volunteered us.

Tracy: Why am I not surprised.

Eccleston: Emma, you're incredible. Oh, before I forget. I need you to sign this.

Emma: Tom, what's this for?

Eccleston: Well, two things. It acknowledges your receipt of the reward the bank put out for the capture of the robber, and second it shows your outstanding loan balance is now at zero.

Emma: That is good news.

{Emma signs a piece of paper}

Eccleston: Thank you.

Bob: {Entering caring a sack of socks} Did I hear you right, I'm on my own now for six months.

Emma: Yes, I'm afraid so. It was the best deal I could sweet talk the judge into.

Bob: Well, so much for my vacation plans.

Eccleston: What do you have there?

Bob: This, my dear sir, is a container holding the answer of one of life's little mysteries.

Eccleston: The cure for the common cold?

Tracy: Not that mysterious.

Bob: It's my collection of missing socks.

Eccleston: Oh, I've always wondered where all the lost socks go.

Emma: They come here, Tom, they come here.

Act 2
Scene 2: Alternate Ending

{It's a short time later. Bob and Tracy enter from the back.}

Tracy: Bob, I don't know if I buy it.

Bob: How's that?

Tracy: I don't know that I buy Swifty's explanation for his weird behavior.

Bob: Well, I admit it's a little far-fetched and all, but you know how it is with young people these days, it's hardly out of the question.

Tracy: Bob, I'm younger than you. How . . .

Bob: {Interrupts Tracy} Not by much.

Tracy: Much. Most people your age, at least the ones I know, are cynical to the point of exasperation or at least skeptical about everything that comes along. How is it you can give Swifty a pass?

Bob: Let me ask you something, Tracy.

Tracy: Okay.

Bob: Have you ever worked for the government?

Tracy: Not directly.

Bob: How about indirectly, I don't care.

Tracy: No. When did you ever work for the government?

Bob: I was in the navy for 20 years. If that ain't government employment, I don't know what is.

Tracy: I don't see where this is going.

Bob: I'll tell you where it's going. The men and women in our military are some of the finest there is, but the bureaucracy that runs the show. Well, let's say, once you've seen how things get done in government, ain't much else that will surprise you.

Tracy: That' bad, huh?

Bob: Makes this situation look like a morning cup of coffee.

Tracy: A morning cup of coffee? {Thinks about it for a second and gives up} If you say so.

Bob: Trust me on this, one. I know what I'm talking about. You can take it to the bank. Hey, that's kind of funny.

Tracy: Oh, please. I'd still feel a lot better if I had some supporting evidence.

Bob: I guess I'm still not seeing what you're seeing.

Tracy: Bob, you're a pretty smart guy. I would think that even you could add two plus two and get four.

Bob: That was using old math. With today's math, two plus two could equal Jimmy gets an extra recess.

Tracy: Well, first, Swifty show's up out of the blue.

Bob: We're a service oriented business, people walk in off the street all of the time.

Tracy: People we don't know.

Bob: Tracy, you and I know just about everybody in this town. I probably know half the people in this county and I imagine Ms. Emma knows slightly more than I do, but that doesn't mean we know everyone.

Tracy: What about the description and the sketch the police did of the suspect?

Bob: You said it yourself, that narrows it down to maybe thirty percent of the county's population. Swifty's a fine looking young man, but he's by no means out of the ordinary. Why when I was his age, I considered myself a mighty handsome fellow.

Tracy: Bob, when you were his age, dinosaurs would have been the only ones that cared.

Bob: I had two for pets. Nice little critters, too. Too bad the ice age had to wipe them out.

Tracy: You're not taking me serious.

Bob: I would if you started making sense. So far nothing you've said to me sets off alarms. You know like burglar alarms. That's another good one.

Tracy: What about the bag?

Bob: You mean his laundry bag?

Tracy: When did they start embossing the letters PRB on laundry sacks.

Bob: PRB could mean anything.

Tracy: Why won't he just show us what's in the bag?

Bob: I don't know, do you like to go around flashing your dirty undies to every stranger that wonders what's in your laundry sack?

Tracy: I haven't been accused of a bank robbery!

Bob: Well, as far as I know, neither has he.

Tracy: What about him jumping into the washing machine?

{Swifty enters from the back room}

Swifty: I'm sorry, I couldn't help but overhear some of what you were saying. I climbed into the washing machine . . . because I was starting to get scared.

Tracy: You see, he must be hiding something.

Swifty: Maybe, but not what you're thinking, I'm sure.

Bob: Then why go take a swim.

Swifty: Look, I have ears and eyes. That cop had been around more than once today. I saw the police sketch. That banker hanging out here. It was all getting a little to nerve racking for me.

Tracy: I understand. The logical thing to do would be to climb inside a giant washing machine.

Swifty: Tracy, please. I need you to believe me.

Bob: Really, kid, you don't need to be worried about those folks. Well, at least not Sandy and Erin. They hang out here just about as much as I do.

Tracy: Sometimes I think they contribute more to the operation of this place.

Bob: I'm just going to ignore that little comment. See here she comes again. {Erin and Chuck enter}

Erin: Okay, I feel like I just entered a prison or something.

Swifty: Oh, great.

Erin: I'm sorry. You all just look so down. Don't be down. It's a wonderful day.

Tracy: Easy for you to say.

Erin: Is everything okay, Swifty?

Swifty: Just go get Ms. Emma and I'll try to explain it all to you. I guess I really don't have a choice.

Tracy: Okay by me. {Starts to exit} Come on, Bob.

Bob: What do you need me for?

Tracy: Just come on. {Side glance made to Erin and Swifty}

Bob: Oh.

{Swifty grabs his laundry bag and comes around and sits down on one of the benches}

Swifty: By the way, I think your rug is done. It looks pretty good.

Erin: Really, that's great. But that's not what I stopped by for.

Swifty: It isn't?

Erin: Charles and I were talking, and we wanted to know if you had any plans for dinner tonight.

Swifty: You and Charles, why?

Erin: Well, we thought maybe you might want to join us?

Swifty: Oh. That's awful nice of you, but . . .

Erin: Oh, I see. Not interested in a girl with a son.

Swifty: No, it's not that at all. It's just, you don't know me and I'm afraid . . .

Erin: But that's the point. How am I supposed to get to know you unless we spend some time together?

Swifty: We're here. You can get to know me here.

Erin: Not at work. I know Ms. Emma, Tracy and Bob are probably the easiest people in the world to get along with, but it would be nice not to have all the distractions.

Swifty: Okay. Would you like me to bring anything?

Erin: {Jokingly} Yeah, if you happen to have million dollars you could always bring that along. {Chuckles at it but Swifty doesn't reciprocate}

Swifty: I'm afraid I don't have that much.

Erin: It was a joke, silly. You don't need to bring anything. Just come and have a good time. I hope you like to play board games. Chuck . . . I mean Charles will insist we play a game.

Swifty: Board games are fine.

Erin: Okay, then. {Stands to leave} We'll see you around seven?

Swifty: {Standing} Wait, I don't know where you live.

Erin: It would take you a long time to find me then, wouldn't it. {Digs in her purse and pulls out a business card} Here's my card. It shouldn't be hard to find. It's just down the street a couple of blocks.

Swifty: Okay, bye. {Erin exits}

{Swifty realizes she forgot her rug and runs over to grab it and runs to the door, but she's out of site}

Tracy: {Entering see's Swifty apparently leaving the laundry} See, he's leaving.

Emma: Swifty, how could you?

Swifty: What?

Bob: I have to admit, Tracy. I really thought you were barking up the wrong, tree, but it looks like the dog treed the right cat.

{Emma, Tracy and Swifty all pause for a second and just stare at Bob}

Tracy: What is that suppose to mean?

Bob: What I'm trying to say, is it looks like you called him out.

Swifty: Really, I can explain.

Emma: Swifty, I really want to help you.

Swifty: You can help by letting me explain.

Emma: God wants me to love you.

Swifty: I want you to love me too, but . . .

Emma: It's difficult in my own power, but with God, I can.

Swifty: Wonderful. Now that we have that settled, may I explain? {Eccleston enters the laundry}

Eccleston: {Eccleston enters and crosses over to Emma} Good afternoon, Ms. Emma, everyone.

Everyone: {In Unison} Hi.

Emma: {Tom takes Emma aside.} Tom, I don't suppose you have any good news for me.

Eccleston: No, I'm afraid I don't. I've exhausted all of my approaches with the board. If I don't get a commitment from you to pay at least five thousand dollars by the end of next week, they're going to start legal proceedings.

Emma: Oh, Tom. I don't know where I'll be able to come up with that kind of money in two weeks. At most I'd be able to come up with half of that.

Eccleston: I know and I'm sorry. I've done all I can. Now if you'll excuse me.

Emma: What's the rush?

Eccleston: Oh, it's this whole robbery thing.

Emma: No luck, huh?

Eccleston: We'll you saw the details we got off of the camera. The police don't have anything at this point. As it is, the robber is probably 2 or 3 states away.

Emma: Oh, he could be closer than you think.

Eccleston: I wish I had your optimism. Anyway, the board has just issued a reward for leads leading to the capture of the crook. It's pretty sizeable.

Emma: Is that really necessary?

Eccleston: They seem to think so. Look, Emma. I just want to remind you that when the inevitable happens, that you know I did all I could. You're one of the nicest, Godliest people I know. I just wish the economy would have worked more in your favor than it did.

Emma: {Smiling} Oh, don't you worry about it. I'm not concerned about me; I'm just worried about Tracy and Bob. I don't know how to help them when the laundry closes down.

Eccleston: Emma, if it's any conciliation, I will do everything I can to help them find a job.

Emma: Really, that would be just darling of you.

Eccleston: Oh, and don't forget to bring those bills down so we can check those out for you.

Emma: I'll try.

Eccleston: {As he passes Swifty} Going somewhere?

Swifty: Not planning on it.

Eccleston: That looks like a pretty heavy bag you got there.

Swifty: It is.

Eccleston: Big enough to hold a body or a whole lot of cash.

Swifty: No, no, nothing like that, just a customer's laundry.

Eccleston: I see.

{Eccleston exits}

Emma: Now where was I?

Bob: You were about to explain how God loves him and so do you.

Emma: Oh yes, thank you Bob.

Swifty: Look, Emma. This is Erin's rug. She stopped by just a few minutes ago, and she left without it.

Emma: Did she? {Looking at Tracy}

Tracy: Yes, she was here.

Swifty: I was going to run it out to her but you guys caught me before I could get out the door.

Bob: Caught being the appropriate word.

Swifty: See for yourself. {Swifty walks the big bag over, and drops it on the floor and opens it up for all to see}

Tracy: It looks like a rug.

Bob: It's most definitely a rug. And, it's mighty clean if I do say so myself.

Swifty: I want to come clean too.

Emma: Let's hear it then.

Swifty: I just inherited a quarter million dollars from Rex Oxnard's estate.

{There is brief silence}

Bob: That's a lot of money.

Tracy: How do we know that's true?

Swifty: {Opening his sack} Its right in here.

{Everyone pears inside}

Emma: He wasn't kidding.

Tracy: How do we know this isn't the bank's money?

Emma: He should have a receipt and papers from an attorney.

Swifty: I should, and I did, but after I had cashed out the check from the estate, I went to the park to think about what I should do next. I'm young and stupid. I wasn't sure. So, as I was sitting there, I managed to lose the folder that contained all of the paperwork. I got scared.

Tracy: So why did you come here?

Swifty: I looked all over for it. I was working my way back to the bank when I stopped in here.

Bob: I don't understand why you stopped here.

Swifty: I had heard the sirens and saw the police outside the bank. At this point, I guess my imagination got a little carried away and I started looking for a place to think. I figured I'd step in here and fill out an application when everything went sideways.

Emma: Explain what you mean by sideways.

Swifty: Well, I didn't expect you to hire me, at least not on the spot. By then I knew the police were out looking and I had no way to explain the money in the bag. I need your help.

Emma: Well, I think I know just the person to help straighten this whole thing out.

{Sandy enters, spots Swifty, and draws her firearm and begins to shout commands}

Sandy: Swifty, don't move. Emma, Bob, Tracy step away. Set the bag down, slowly, Swifty and put your hands on your head. {Swifty complies}

Emma: Sandy, I think we have a misunderstanding.

Sandy: Not now, Emma. Swifty, you have the right to remain silent. Anything you say can and will be used against you in a court of law. {Sandy lowers her weapon and approaches him with handcuffs, and begins to cuff him}

Tracy: What are you arresting him for?

Sandy: For the robbery of the People's Republic Bank.

Tracy: How much was stolen?

Sandy: Around five thousand dollars.

Tracy: I bet if you look in that bag, you'll see that bag doesn't contain five thousand dollars.

Sandy: There is money in that bag, I know it.

Tracy: Yes, there's money, but not the money from the robbery.

Sandy: What? Let me see that bag. {Sandy takes the bag and quickly scans the contents} I guess you're right. There's a lot more than that in there. {To Swifty} Where'd you get that money?

Swifty: I inherited it from Rex Oxnard.

Sandy: No, I mean, where did you get it?

Swifty: From the People Republic Bank, across town.

Sandy: When?

Swifty: Early this morning. Right after the hearing and the presentation of the check from the estate's attorney.

Sandy: Where's the documents you received from the estate and the receipt?

Swifty: That's a problem. I've lost them.

Sandy: Uh, huh.

Emma: Really, Sandy, I believe him.

Sandy: It doesn't matter; I'm going to have to take you in for questioning.

Bob: Hey, look everybody, there's a newsflash coming on the TV.

Tracy: Bob, turn up the sound.

{Bob reaches over and grabs the TV remote}

TV Announcer: Police have just announced that they have captured a suspect in the Republic Bank robbery, just moments ago. The suspect was apprehended after being pulled over for a speeding violation. The officer recognized the suspect from the sketch that went out earlier, and when the suspect decided to flee on foot, the officer captured the suspect with a bag of cash. The alleged robber is now in the county jail awaiting his preliminary hearing. The bag was said to contain all of the missing ten thousand dollars that had been stolen from the People's Republic ATM earlier this morning.

Tracy: I guess that clears that up.

Sandy: Not so fast. There's still a question about this money.

Emma: We can be civilized about this. Surely we can go down to the attorney's office and/or the bank and someone can surely testify to seeing this young man legally received this cash.

Swifty: Excuse me, since you have my money in hand and the police have purportedly captured the real robber, could you at least release me from these handcuffs. I'll go wherever you want to go to help clear this up.

Sandy: I suppose that's reasonable given the circumstances.

{Sandy works the lock on the handcuffs and releases Swifty. He rubs his wrists gently}

Swifty: Thank you.

Sandy: Come on, I'll drive you across town.

Swifty: Just a minute. {To Emma} Emma, are you really going to lose this place?

Emma: Yes, I'm afraid it's probably going to come to that, unless God intervenes.

Swifty: I don't know if God can help you, but I might be willing too.

Emma: Swifty, I can't take your money, it wouldn't be right.

Swifty: How are you going to help your friends if you can't take care of yourself?

Emma: God will work it all out.

Swifty: Why do you have such a positive outlook? Everything you have will be gone in just a few days. Your business, your income, your life as you've known it will be over.

Emma: We all have our opportunities given by God to do the right thing – His way – or the wrong thing – our way. I have done, what I've done to please God. If it's time for me to give up the Sock, then I'll just have to find out what's next on God's plan for me. We all have a choice. You have a choice, and it starts with accepting who God is, and what He can do for you.

Swifty: Even a messed up kid, like me?

Emma: Swifty, God specializes in taking things that are broken, and making them better than new. That's what he does. You better scoot.

Swifty: When we get this all cleared up, maybe you'll consider taking me on as a partner.

Emma: {Smiling} It's an opportunity I'm willing to consider, what do you two think?

Tracy: Sure.

Bob: I think that's a wonderful idea.

Swifty: {Starts to head out, turns back} I've always wondered where all the lost socks go, and now I think I know the answer.

{Lights Fade. End Act 2 Scene 2 – Alternate Ending}

{The End}

Appendix A
Activities

This section contains suggested activities that can be incorporated into the production should you choose to make this an interactive evening. It is suggested that the cast assist with the activities as much as possible, but not to do more than one or two between scenes. A meal may also be incorporated as a dinner theatre option. Since this play is designed as a stand-alone production, the items suggested can be incorporated at the director/producers discretion.

Games:

Sock Mismatch: Everyone is familiar with this routine. Who has hasn't had basket of mismatched socks that needed paired up and put together. In this game, each table is given a basket of unmatched socks - depending on the size of the table.

> 4 person table – 8 pairs
> 8 person table – 12 pairs
> 10 person table – 16 pairs

The object of the game is the table that matches the socks first wins.

Tweaks: These are optional tweaks to the game that can make for more excitement.

1.) Have a cast member deliver the basket just before the game starts
2.) Have one or more mismatch in a separate basket at a different table
3.) Have one of the mismatch socks as part of the stage decoration and award a special prize to the table or person that discovers it.

Clothes Basket-ball: The audience will need to take a pair of socks (that match) and ball them up and shoot them into an awaiting basket. The trick is a cast member will be holding the basket and must be at least 6 feet away from the table. More than one pair of socks should be present on the table; however, not everyone has to shoot the shots into the basket. Rebounds will be handled by the cast member holding the basket and should be returned to the table. First table to successfully shoot all of their socks into the basket wins.

Washing machine Relay: A table is set at one end of the room. The object of the game is for each table to go hurry to the table which contains a sock and a bucket along with a small amount of soap and softener. There are six activities that have to be performed by the audience. In between each activity the participant must run back to the table and select the next participant.

Each station should include the following for the game: a small bucket (like a one gallon ice cream pail), Dixie cup with soap, three Dixie cups of water, Dixie cup softener, and hair dryer.

1. Load the laundry. (Put the sock in the bucket)
2. Add Soap and wash. (1 Dixie cup of water plus soap)
3. Rinse. (1 Dixie cup of water)
4. Softener. (Dixie cup of softener)
5. Rinse. (1 Dixie cup of water)
6. Dry. (blow dry the sock with the hair dryer)

ABOUT THE AUTHOR

Matthew Graphman is a twenty year veteran in the information technology world. He studied writing and drama, as well as computers while attending Bob Jones University in the late 80's and early 90's. In school, he was involved in more than 9 productions including the university's production of Shakespeare's "The Taming of the Shrew". Since then, he has written several one acts, a musical, numerous sketches used for vacation bible school, two novels and several children's books. He met his wife, Wendy, of twenty-five years in college and started a family shortly after graduating in 1991. He currently resides in Bloomington, Indiana with his wife and two youngest children, Kathryn (Kat) and Ethan. He continues to write, direct and produce dramas in his local church, and believes that God uses the medium of drama to encourage the saints and challenge the lost.

Printed in the United States
By Bookmasters